the POWER book

What is it, Who has it, and Why?

First published in the UK in 2019 by

Ivy Kids

An imprint of The Quarto Group

The Old Brewery

6 Blundell Street

London N7 9BH

United Kingdom

www.QuartoKnows.com

A CIP record for this book is available from the Library of Congress.

ISBN: 978-1-78240-927-4

This book was conceived, designed, & produced by

Ivy Kids

58 West Street, Brighton BN1 2RA, United Kingdom

PUBLISHER David Breuer

IN-HOUSE TEAM Susie Behar, Hannah Dove,
Kate Haynes, & Lucy Menzies

ART DIRECTOR Hanri van Wyk

PROJECT EDITOR Claire Saunders

DESIGNERS Claire Munday & Suzie Harrison

Manufactured in Singapore CO072019

1 3 5 7 9 10 8 6 4 2

the POWER book

WRITTEN BY

**Claire Saunders,
Hazel Songhurst,
Georgia Amson-Bradshaw,
Minna Salami &
Mik Scarlet**

ILLUSTRATED BY

Joelle Avelino & David Broadbent

CONTENTS

Power to
the people!

Rights
for
women!

PEACE!

we ALL have power!

FOREWORD BY ROXANE GAY

When I was a kid, I hated being told what to do. I had to wake up and go to bed when my parents told me to. I had to do my chores and go to school and do my homework and keep my room clean. I had to stop teasing my brothers and come home before dark when I was playing outside. At school, my teachers were also telling me what to do, and when. I had little control over my world and it felt very unfair.

The older I got, the more I came to understand that in hating being told what to do, I was really hating how little power I had and how much power so many people had over me. I came to understand that power, in part, was about being able to have control—of my time, my body, how I lived.

Roxane Gay is an author who writes about things that matter to her. Her books are read by thousands of people and her words can affect the way her readers think about important issues in society—this is an awesome form of power.

We deal with all kinds of power in this world. There is personal power—the power we have (or don't) in our day-to-day lives and the choices we make for ourselves. There is economic power—the power that comes with money and what we do with it. And, of course, there is political power—the power we have when we vote, when we speak up about what we care about, when we protest things we think are wrong. This is the power our government representatives have as they make laws and govern the countries we live in.

It is important to understand power and the different ways in which power can shape our lives. It is important to understand what it means to have power and what it means to not have power. Sometimes power is used for good and sometimes it is used in terrible ways—but power, in and of itself, is neither good nor bad.

There is a saying that is more than two hundred years old—"power tends to corrupt and absolute power corrupts absolutely." What that means is all too often, when people have power, they can sometimes do bad things with it. And when someone has too much power, and there is no one who challenges that power, they can do a lot of harm.

But maybe, if more people understand power, they will be better able to handle the responsibility. In this book, you will learn about power, what it means to have power, and what you can do with your power to create change for yourself and the people you care about. No matter who or how old you are, you can create change in this world we live in.

INTRODUCTION

If a person has power, it means that they can make things happen in the way that they want. Power is neither good nor bad; it totally depends on how it is used. It can be used well (like when your parents who love you ask you to stop eating all the marshmallows in the house and go to bed before 2 a. m.). It can be used badly (like when your so-called friend threatens to tell everyone your secret, unless you steal something from the store).

Many different people, from leaders to teachers to parents to you, have power. In this book, you can find out about all the different types of power people have, and why some people don't have the power that others have. You'll learn about some amazing people who tried to change their lives and the lives of others for the better by changing the rules of power.

By the end of this book, you'll have built up a power-spotting visor that will allow you to see this invisible force. Maybe, you too can become a force for good when you learn about and use your own personal power!

"Humanity owes the child
the best it has to give."

Eglantyne Jebb (1876–1928)

EVERYDAY POWER

Everyday power is all around you, all the time, although you might not always realize it's there. It's what influences your relationships with your friends, parents, and teachers, and it's what determines how you spend your time.

One easy way to spot it is to think of all the rules you have to follow, from brushing your teeth to doing your homework or cleaning up your room. Everyone has to follow rules—parents, teachers, doctors, the police, and so on. Some rules apply to everyone, others apply to specific people or situations. But all rules are to do with power, and they show us that power, and who has it, can **CHANGE**.

In this chapter we describe how everyday power affects our lives, so that you can learn to recognize it, understand it, and hopefully grow your own power.

ADULTS RULE!

How do you feel about the fact
that, at home and at school,
the adults call the shots?

Every day we have to follow rules about things, like what time we have to be at school, what we have to wear, how we should behave, and who we have to listen to. It can be pretty boring! But who makes these rules? And why?

In all areas of our lives, the rules that we follow are made by people with power. In school, teachers have power. At home, parents have power. This means these adults get to tell you what to do, whether that's not talking in class or going to bed at a certain time. The power your parents have also means they get to make important decisions for you, such as which school you go to, where you live, and what you eat. Having to follow the rules that adults make can be frustrating, and can often seem unfair.

Unfortunately, kids don't get to tell adults what to do! The **power balance** is unequal: adults have more power, children have less.

Mostly, adults set rules in order to keep children safe, or to help them become healthy, happy adults. For example, sending you to bed on time means you get a good night's sleep so you stay healthy. Making you do your homework helps you do well at school, so that when you're older you can go to college or get a good job, which will make your life easier as an adult.

Just because adults have the power, it doesn't mean they are always in the right. Adults should never use their power over children to hurt them physically or emotionally, which is very wrong. Although this harmful use of power does happen, most adults will always do what they believe is best for children.

! If you are affected by any of these issues, turn to page 63 for advice.

THE WOMAN WHO STOOD UP FOR CHILDREN

"I believe we should claim certain rights for children."

Eglantyne Jebb was born in 1876 to a well-off family. During World War I, she set up the charity Save the Children, to provide aid to the many children in Europe who were starving. However, she soon realized that more than charity was needed to make certain that children around the world lived happy, healthy lives. In 1923 she drafted the Declaration of the Rights of the Child, an important legal document that stated that all children had the right to food and shelter, and to be protected from exploitation. It was adopted by the international governmental organization, the League of Nations, and later a longer version was agreed by the United Nations (read more about the United Nations on page 23). Eglantyne's work forms the basis of international law that protects children's rights to this day.

THINKING POINT

The age at which a child legally becomes an adult varies from country to country, ranging from 15 to 21. What age do you think it should be?

POWER IN THE PLAYGROUND

Why do some kids get to be
king of the castle?

Are there any bullies in your school? How about cool kids that everyone looks up to? Imbalances of power don't just exist between adults and children. Some kids can have more power than other kids, too.

There are lots of reasons why one child might have more power than another. A difference in age can create an unequal power balance. An older child might have more knowledge or experience, and so be admired by other kids. Another reason might simply be that one kid is bigger. Having more physical strength could give someone the power to force a less physically-strong person to do something, through the threat of violence, or actual violence.

When one person repeatedly hurts another person on purpose, that is **bullying**. Bullying can be emotional, such as always leaving someone out or calling them names, as well as physical. Bullying involves a power imbalance: the bully has more power and the victim has less (or, at least, the victim and bully believe that to be the case).

Unfortunately, some of the things that can affect the power that adults have, such as their gender, race, or ability, can also affect children. Read more about this in "What Affects a Person's Power?," starting on page 32.

 If you are affected by any of these issues, turn to page 63 for advice.

It isn't just through nasty behavior like bullying that you can see power imbalances among kids and teens. Have you ever looked at another person and wished you could be more like them? When someone is popular and looked up to, they have power to influence other people's behavior. Famous people have this sort of power. People want to be like them, and this means that they can influence what people wear, say, do, or even believe through their own actions and choices.

THE BULLIED GIRL WHO FOUND FAME

Sometimes, people who go on to become famous and popular have a rough time at school because they are a bit different. **Taylor Swift** started writing songs aged 12, when she was being bullied and left out by the other kids at her school. Nowadays, Taylor Swift is one of the most popular singers in the world, and what she says can have a big influence on the millions of fans who look up to her. In 2018, when she tweeted to her fans encouraging them to sign up to vote in the US midterm elections, 65,000 people registered to vote in just 24 hours.

THINKING POINT

Do you have any brothers or sisters, cousins or friends who are a different age from you? Who do you think has the most power in your relationship?

WHO'S IN CHARGE OF THE GROWN-UPS?

Even the **boss** has a **boss.**

With adults telling you what to do all the time, it's easy to forget that they have to follow lots of rules, too. There are other adults who have more power than they do, and get to boss them around. Even really important people, such as presidents or prime ministers, still have to obey the law!

One place where adults will often experience someone having more power than them is at work.

For people who work with others in a company or organization, there is usually a **hierarchy.** This means that the people who work there have different levels of power and responsibility within the organization, perhaps with a single person at the top.

BOSS

MANAGERS

EMPLOYEES

Hierarchies exist in all sorts of groups and organizations, such as governments (where a president or prime minister is at the top), the Catholic church (where the Pope is at the top) and the army (headed by a general). And just as there can be an imbalance of power between one child and another, the same is true for adults, too.

Another thing that has power over adults is the state. The state is what we call all the organizations that are needed to run a country. It includes the government, but also things such as the police and the justice system, including lawyers, law courts, and prisons. If you break a rule at school, you might be punished by a teacher. If an adult is caught breaking the law by the police, they are punished by the justice system. Learn more about governments in the next chapter.

THE MAN WHO WANTED TO GET RID OF THE STATE

Throughout history, there have been many people and groups who have wanted to change society so that all people are equal, and not under the power of a state. The idea of a society organized without hierarchies and without a government is called "anarchism." One of the first groups to try to create an anarchist society were the so-called Diggers in England in the 17th century, led by Gerrard Winstanley. He believed that no person should have the right to rule over another, and that if you got rid of the state and its laws, everyone would naturally cooperate with one another and live happily. The Diggers set up a small farming community on a hillside in southern England, but local landowners repeatedly attacked it and the community was abandoned after just 18 months.

THINKING POINT

What do you think would happen if we got rid of government and the state?

Do you think it would be a good thing or a bad thing?

"I am not interested in power for power's sake, but I'm interested in power that is moral, that is right, and that is good."

Martin Luther King Jr. (1929-1968)

WORLD-CHANGING POWER

World-changing power is the power that governs countries, starts wars and revolutions, spreads big ideas, and changes things from the top.

This power can do great good or terrible evil in the world. It can turn people's lives upside down, separate families, and lead to children living in poverty. Or, it can end suffering, unite nations, and defeat injustice.

In this chapter, we look at different examples of this awesome power, from royal rulers to radical rebels. By the end of it, you will be armed with some impressive knowledge to help you understand the world a bit better. Once you know more about how it works, you'll discover ways to CHALLENGE power if you want to, and stand up for what you believe in.

LEADERS

Powerful kings, queens, and emperors once ruled over us, but **ordinary citizens** can become leaders in **today's world.**

There are many different types of leader. There are leaders of schools, armies, governments, and religions. **Can these leaders do whatever they want? Are they completely in charge?** No, no one is completely in charge, but some leaders have more power than others.

For example, there are various systems of government in different countries. In a **democracy**, the government is made up of people who have been voted for, or elected, by the citizens, giving the citizens a say in how their country is run. In many countries, the head of the government is the president or prime minister. Governments hold a lot of power, but it is hard for most leaders to do whatever they want. An unpopular action—such as raising taxes—may lose them their citizens' support and lessen their power.

The opposite system is known as an **autocracy**, in which one person, such as a dictator or a monarch, holds all the power and the citizens have no say.

Many people believe that if one person or one group has too much power, they will use their power unwisely, and not act in a way that really helps people. And, just because you have power over people, it doesn't make you a good leader.

NAPOLÉON BONAPARTE

Napoléon was a great general who became Emperor of France from 1804 to 1814. Despite all his power, when he began to lose military campaigns, he was forced into exile.

QUEEN ELIZABETH I

This Queen of England ruled from 1558 to 1603, and under her reign England became more powerful. Although adored by her people, she was capable of the cruel act of beheading her cousin to stay in power.

THE DALAI LAMA

The Dalai Lama is the spiritual leader of Tibetan Buddhism. Although he doesn't have any political power, the Tibetan people respect his ideas and opinions, and consider him their leader.

You don't have to be famous to be a leader. There are leaders in all walks of life. Your teacher, for example, is a leader.

HERE ARE SOME QUALITIES THAT A GOOD LEADER SHOULD HAVE:

- Honesty
- The ability to inspire others
- Being able to communicate well
- Being a good decision-maker.

THE MAN WHO WAS KNOWN AS THE "FATHER" OF INDIA

"In a gentle way, you can shake the world."

Mohandas Gandhi (1869–1948) led the Indian nation to independence from British rule. He wanted Indians to rule India. Gandhi was vegetarian and he believed in non-violence toward living things. He didn't want to fight the British. Instead, he led peaceful protests but, despite this, he was arrested and spent nine months in prison. Gandhi was supported by many people across the world and, in 1947, India became independent from Britain. It was split into two countries, India and Pakistan. Gandhi was known as the Father of the Nation, and was given the name "Mahatma," which means "Great Soul."

THINKING POINT

Do you think YOU would make a good leader? Of all the people you know, who do you think would make the best leader? Why?

WHAT IS WAR FOR?

War is a **deadly battle**
for power between nations.

Mao Zedong, the leader of China
from 1949 to 1976, once said:
**"Whoever has an army has power,
and war decides everything."**
For thousands of years, nations
have sent their armies to war in
order to win more power—or
to stop others from having too
much of it.

WHY MIGHT A COUNTRY DECIDE TO GO TO WAR?

- To seize more land for its people to live on or for growing food.

- To steal the wealth of another country, for example, its precious
  minerals or oil.

- To show it is better and more powerful than other countries.

- To fight another country that does not share its beliefs
  (such as religion or politics).

- To remove a tyrant from power.

- To defend itself from possible attack.

Another way that countries grabbed land and power in
the past was through **colonization**. This is when a country
(normally a rich, powerful one) takes over another, less powerful
part of the world and turns it into a "colony" under their control.
The ancient Greek and Roman empires had lots of colonies. More
recently, many European countries did, too. From the 16th century onwards,
Britain, France, Spain, and other European powers set up colonies all over
the world, from Asia to the Americas to Africa. The invading country
usually took advantage of the colony's resources and forced the people
living there to obey its rules.

Wars have become more and more deadly throughout history as humans have developed more powerful weapons. In World War II, over **70 million people** died—that's about 3 out of every 100 people alive in the world at that time.

It is governments and nations that decide to go to war, but it is **ordinary people who suffer** in them. Many of the people who die in wars aren't soldiers, but civilians (nonsoldiers) killed by disease or starvation. These civilians have no power at all. They didn't start the war and may not even agree with the reasons it is being fought. And they have no power to end it.

THINKING POINT

For thousands of years people have argued about what, if anything, makes a war "just" (meaning "right" and "fair"). Do you think some wars can be justified?

THE ORGANIZATION THAT TRIES TO KEEP THE PEACE

After the terrible loss of life in World War II, the winning nations formed an organization called the **United Nations (UN)**. The main aim of the UN was to keep world peace and try to prevent terrible wars like World War II from ever happening again. When the UN was founded, it had 51 member states. Now there are 193 member states—virtually all of the countries in the world.

The UN works to improve people's lives, help prevent wars, and encourage fighting countries to make peace. But if peace talks don't work, the UN also has the power to use armed force, if it thinks it is necessary—for example, if one country has illegally invaded another.

VOTING

Voting puts **power** into the hands of the **people!**

Have you ever voted for anything? Voting is when **people are given a choice** between different options, and the option chosen by the most people wins.

Around the world, people use their vote in elections to decide how their country will be run. They listen to the promises made by different political parties, and decide which issues are important to them. Then they vote for a party to represent their views and act on their behalf. Politicians have to be careful about making promises they can't keep; if they get elected and don't keep their promises, the people might not vote for them next time!

In some countries, where power is held in the hands of one person, people don't always get to vote for who leads their country. Sometimes, elections might be held, but these are not always run fairly.

In most countries, you don't have to vote if you don't want to, and some people don't bother. Other countries think voting is so important that they have made it against the law not to vote.

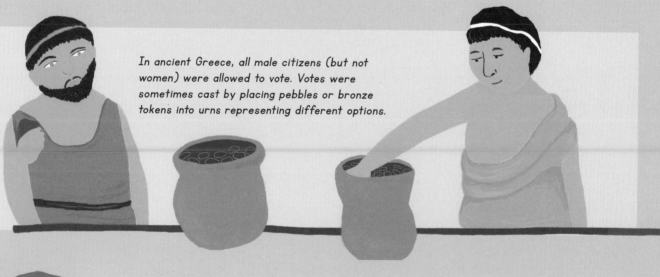

In ancient Greece, all male citizens (but not women) were allowed to vote. Votes were sometimes cast by placing pebbles or bronze tokens into urns representing different options.

Today, most people vote by putting a cross or a mark on a ballot paper. Votes are secret, so that no one knows how anyone else voted.

WHO GETS TO VOTE?

The right to vote is called **suffrage**. Today, most countries around the world allow all adult citizens to vote. But that hasn't always been the case. In the past, countries have stopped people from voting because of their race, gender, religion, or how much education they had. Even today, some countries don't allow certain people to vote. These people include:

● Prisoners

● Those with a disability

● Those in the police and army.

Do you agree with these rules?

THE WOMAN WHO FOUGHT FOR HER RIGHT TO VOTE

"Deeds, not words!"

In the early 20th century, women in many countries were not allowed to vote. **Emmeline Pankhurst** was a leader of the British suffrage movement, which fought to give women the same voting rights as men. Pankhurst, her daughters Christabel and Sylvia, and other women in the movement were known as suffragettes. The suffragette protests were often violent. The women smashed windows, set fire to buildings, and let off bombs. Pankhurst and others were sent to prison, where they went on hunger strike. After World War I ended in 1918, some women were given the vote, but it took until 1928, the year Pankhurst died, for all women in Britain to win the same voting rights as men.

THINKING POINT

Different countries have different rules about what age a person can start voting. For most countries it's somewhere between 16 and 21 years. At what age do you think young people should be allowed to vote?

PEOPLE POWER

It isn't just leaders that have power.
You have it, too!

Voting is one way people can influence how their country is run. But it's not the only way. If people are unhappy about something, they can join together to protest against it and try to change things. This could be a protest against the actions of a government—for example, people might disagree with their country's decision to go to war. Or it could be a protest about the unfair way a particular group of people is treated by society.

People can protest in many different ways. These include:

Peaceful **marches** and **demonstrations**. Some of the biggest protest marches around the world have involved many hundreds of thousands of people marching through the streets or countryside.

Raising awareness of issues through **social media**. This is a powerful way to spread a message to millions of people.

"Civil disobedience." This is when a group of citizens peacefully refuses to obey the laws or demands of a government, to try to persuade the government to change the way it does things.

"Boycotting." This means not buying certain products because you disagree with the company that makes them or the way they are made. This could be, for example, not buying clothes that have been made using child labor.

Power to the people!

PEACE!

Rights for women!

NO WAR!

ARE YOU A CHANGEMAKER?

Someone who campaigns for change is known as an **activist**. All through history, ordinary people have challenged unfair systems and campaigned to change society. Activists have fought for the ideas they believed would make the world a better place for themselves and others. Their actions made them famous and we remember them today.

I'm an activist

ACTIVIST

THE WOMAN WHO REFUSED TO GIVE UP HER SEAT ON A BUS

"You must never be fearful about what you are doing when it is right."

In 1955, in Montgomery, Alabama, USA, African-American **Rosa Parks** refused to give up her bus seat to a white man. It was a brave act—she was arrested for breaking the city's racial segregation laws, which kept black and white people separate. Parks belonged to a movement that supported racial equality, and a group of civil rights activists, led by church minister Martin Luther King Jr., boycotted the bus company in protest. A year later, the Supreme Court decided that segregated seating on buses was unjust. This victory inspired the US civil rights movement, which eventually ended segregation across America.

THINKING POINT

"You must be the change you want to see in the world."
Mohandas Gandhi

What do you think of this statement?

WORD POWER

Words can change the world!

Have you ever heard the phrase **"knowledge is power?"** It's true. The more you know, the more power you have to make good decisions. That is why learning and working hard at school helps you to do well in life when you are older.

Today, information is all around us—in books, on TV, websites, and social media. But that wasn't always the case. In the Middle Ages, knowledge was only found in books, which were written out by hand. This meant they were rare and expensive, and no one except rich people and the powerful, wealthy church could afford them.

When the **printing press** was invented in Europe in the 15th century, everything changed. Suddenly, books could be made quickly and cheaply, and ordinary people could afford them. As more people learned to read, they began to question what they were being told by the people in charge. Over time, power moved away from rich people and the church toward ordinary people.

The words and ideas in some books have been so powerful that they have **changed the world.** Books have spread new ways of thinking, sparked violent revolutions, and helped to bring about changes to society.

UNCLE TOM'S CABIN

American Harriet Beecher Stowe's best-selling novel, published in 1852, told the story of Uncle Tom, a black slave. It helped to change attitudes and end slavery in the US.

THE COMMUNIST MANIFESTO

This book, written by Germans Karl Marx and Friedrich Engels in 1848, argued that revolution would create a society where everyone was equal. The ideas in it inspired the Russian Revolution of 1917 and have influenced people around the world.

Today, a lot of the information we read comes from the media (that's TV, newspapers, radio, websites, social media, and ads). What we read or listen to can have a big influence on what we think, which makes the media very powerful.

THINKING
POINT

We trust the media to tell us the truth. Do you think we can always believe everything we read and hear?

Sometimes, a state can use the media to influence what people think by controlling what they read or hear. This can be through **propaganda**, which is biased (one-sided) information. Or it can be through **censorship**, which is when people aren't allowed to read or listen to things that the state doesn't want them to.

THE MAN WHO HAD A DREAM

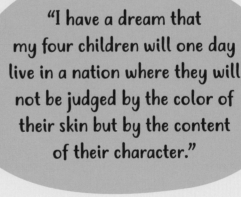

"I have a dream that my four children will one day live in a nation where they will not be judged by the color of their skin but by the content of their character."

It's not just written words that have power. Spoken words can have power, too. One of the most famous speeches ever made was by **Martin Luther King Jr.**, an African-American activist who fought to give people of all races the same rights. In 1963, he helped organize a huge demonstration, where he gave his great "I have a dream" speech. His words and actions helped to bring about the Civil Rights Act the following year, which banned discrimination against people because of their race. King was assassinated in 1968, but his powerful words live on.

REBEL POWER

A rebel is someone who asks,
"Why?"

Rebels don't just accept things the way they are. They question what they see around them, and ask if it is right or fair. They don't follow the rules, or care about what other people might think of them. They are brave enough to go against the flow, and to fight for what they believe in. Rebels can change things.

Throughout history, many rebels have stood up to leaders or governments to fight for greater freedom for groups of people who didn't have power, for example, women, slaves, or people living in poverty. Other rebels have tried to change people's beliefs with an idea that was new or revolutionary for the time.

When enough people rebel, it can bring down governments or monarchies. In the French Revolution in the late 18th century, for example, the people overthrew the king and took control of the country.

GALILEO GALILEI

The 16th-century Italian astronomer Galileo was arrested for arguing that Earth orbited the Sun. This went against the powerful Catholic Church, which taught that Earth was the center of the universe.

SPARTACUS

The famous rebel Spartacus was a gladiator who escaped and helped to lead a group of slaves in an uprising against the mighty Roman Empire. His army had many victories against the Romans before it was finally defeated.

MANAL AL-SHARIF

Many women in Saudi Arabia rebelled against a rule forbidding them from driving. In 2011, Manal al-Sharif was arrested after she posted a video on social media of herself driving. Saudi Arabian women eventually won the right to drive in 2018.

ARE YOU A REBEL? TAKE THE TEST.

● Would you do something you thought was right, even if you knew it would make you unpopular with your friends? Yes/No

● Do you look at the world around you and see things that you would like to change? Yes/No

● Do you sometimes question what you are told to do, if you think it's not right or fair? Yes/No

● Do you stand up for other people who are treated unfairly? Yes/No

If you answered "Yes" to three or more questions, you have the makings of a rebel.

REBEL

THE DOCTOR WHO BECAME A REBEL

"The revolution is not an apple that falls when it is ripe. You have to make it fall."

One of the most famous rebels of all time, **Che Guevara** was born in 1928 in Argentina, where he studied to be a doctor. While traveling around South and Central America, he saw a lot of poor people being treated unfairly. He decided that the only way to change things was through violent revolution. He helped revolutionaries in Cuba seize power in 1959, and he tried to start revolutions in other countries, too, before he was killed. People have different opinions about Che Guevara. Some people think he is a hero who defended the poor, while others see him as a murderer who executed people without trial.

THINKING POINT

Many rebels and rebellions have used violence to overthrow power and make change. Do you think this can be justified?

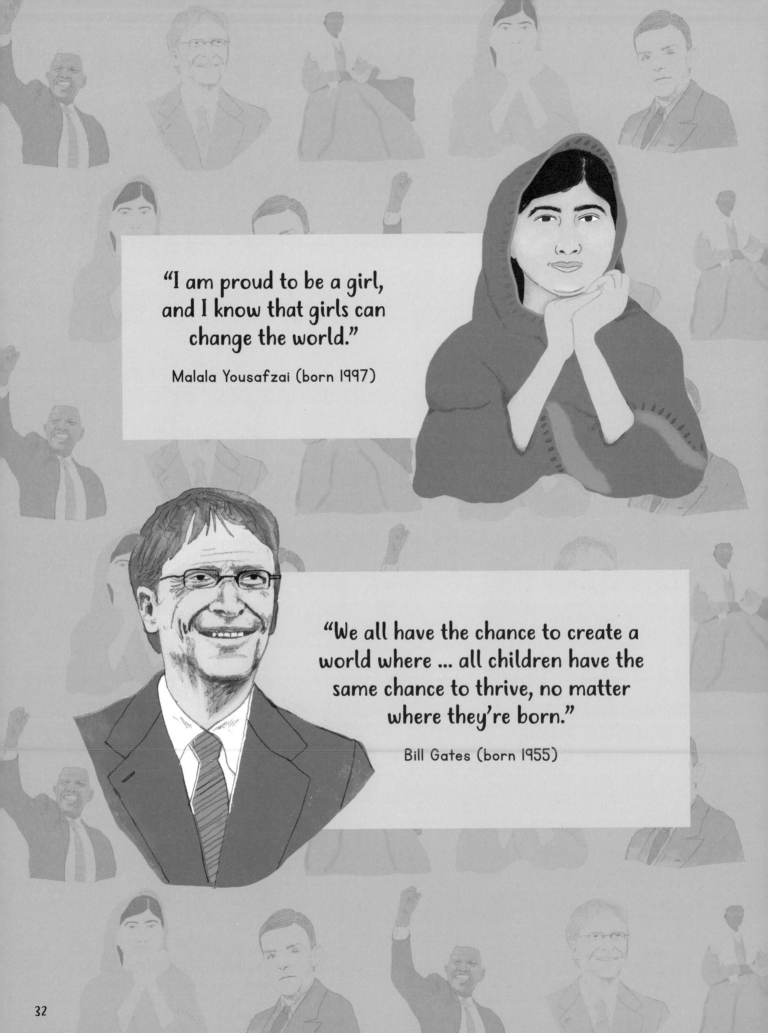

"I am proud to be a girl, and I know that girls can change the world."

Malala Yousafzai (born 1997)

"We all have the chance to create a world where ... all children have the same chance to thrive, no matter where they're born."

Bill Gates (born 1955)

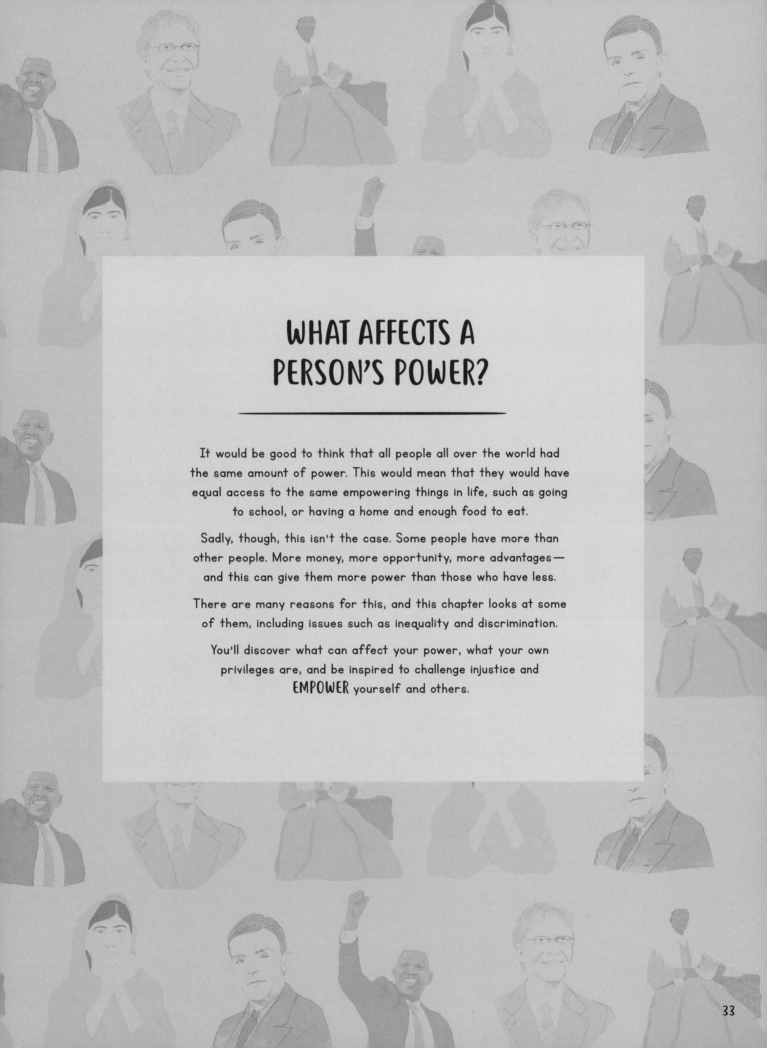

WHAT AFFECTS A PERSON'S POWER?

It would be good to think that all people all over the world had the same amount of power. This would mean that they would have equal access to the same empowering things in life, such as going to school, or having a home and enough food to eat.

Sadly, though, this isn't the case. Some people have more than other people. More money, more opportunity, more advantages— and this can give them more power than those who have less.

There are many reasons for this, and this chapter looks at some of them, including issues such as inequality and discrimination.

You'll discover what can affect your power, what your own privileges are, and be inspired to challenge injustice and **EMPOWER** yourself and others.

WORLD VIEWS

Different people have different views.

What is a "world view"? It's the way that a person sees the world, made up of their **ideas, beliefs, and feelings** about what is right and wrong.

Everybody's world view is different. For example, when it comes to the question of migration (people moving from one country to another), people have very different views. Some people think there should be a limit to how many people can enter a country, while others believe that people should have the right to move to whichever country they choose.

Have you ever wondered where your beliefs and views come from? Some of our beliefs come from what has happened in our own lives, but often the things that we think are right or wrong are shaped by other things, such as what our parents think, the religion we follow, or the culture we live in.

THINKING
POINT

People in the past held many views and beliefs that we disagree with today. Can you think of anything that people think is ok today but that people in the future may think is not ok?

Between the 16th and 19th centuries, over 11 million Africans were kidnapped from their countries and sent on ships across the Atlantic Ocean to be sold into slavery in the Americas. The people who carried out this horrible slave trade justified their actions by their religious views, which said that the black race was not as good as the white race. This was their **world view**.

The enslavement of African people still has an impact on the lives of African-heritage people around the world today. But the example of slavery also shows that while it can take a long time to change people's beliefs and values, it is not impossible. Today, although modern slavery still exists in many forms, most people around the world agree that slavery is wrong and it is illegal in every country.

THE WOMAN WHO HELPED TO CHANGE PEOPLE'S WORLD VIEWS

"Children, who made your skin white? Was it not God? Who made mine black? Was it not the same God?"

In 1797 in the US, Sojourner Truth was born into slavery. At the age of nine, she was separated from her parents when she was sold for $100 to a new owner. In 1826, she escaped and later became an important abolitionist—meaning someone who works to end slavery. She organized protests, gave speeches, brought legal cases to court, and petitioned (sent requests to) the US government. She even met with President Abraham Lincoln to argue not only for the ending of slavery, but also for racial equality and women's rights. Her work, and that of other abolitionists, helped to change people's views, and slavery was finally abolished in the US in 1865.

RACISM

No person, race, or culture is better than another.

Racism is when someone thinks their own race is superior to (or better than) other people's. The most common type of racism is when white people believe they are superior to people who have darker skin than them.

Racism has many terrible consequences. During the hundreds of years that the **slave trade** lasted, millions of black people were enslaved and bought, sold, or killed by white people. More recently, from the 1940s to the 1990s in South Africa, the white ruling class had a system called **apartheid**, in which black and white people were separated. The white people had the best housing, education, and jobs, and black people had a limited right to vote in elections.

WHITES ONLY

Between the 16th and 19th centuries, millions of Africans were captured and shipped across the Atlantic to work as slaves in plantations in the Americas. Many died on the journey.

Under the apartheid system in South Africa, which lasted from 1948 to the early 1990s, white people had their own beaches, transportation, movie theaters, restaurants, and even hospitals that black people were not allowed to use.

Indian South Africans also suffered from racism during apartheid. They had to stay in designated living areas and were not allowed to move freely. Many Indian South Africans played an important part in protesting and changing the injustice of apartheid.

Racism still affects people all over the world today. People are still discriminated against because of their skin color or because they have different cultural or ethnic backgrounds.

Equal rights for all

Indian South Africans against apartheid

People have always fought to end racism. For example, when an innocent seventeen-year-old black teenager named Trayvon Martin was killed by a police officer in Sanford, Florida, in 2012, because of his race, his murder led to a huge anti-racism movement called #BlackLivesMatter, which eventually became a worldwide movement.

We can all help to fight racism, too, by treating everyone with fairness and respect, and speaking out if we see anyone using racist actions or words.

THE MAN WHO INSPIRED A NATION

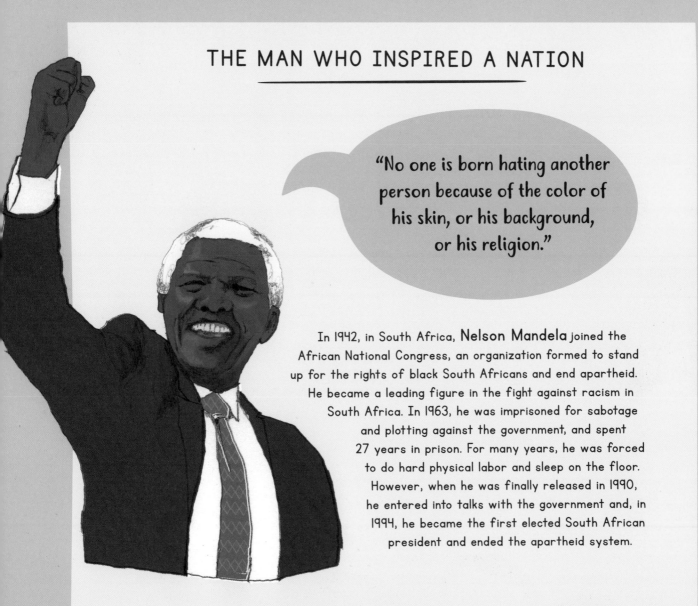

"No one is born hating another person because of the color of his skin, or his background, or his religion."

In 1942, in South Africa, **Nelson Mandela** joined the African National Congress, an organization formed to stand up for the rights of black South Africans and end apartheid. He became a leading figure in the fight against racism in South Africa. In 1963, he was imprisoned for sabotage and plotting against the government, and spent 27 years in prison. For many years, he was forced to do hard physical labor and sleep on the floor. However, when he was finally released in 1990, he entered into talks with the government and, in 1994, he became the first elected South African president and ended the apartheid system.

THINKING POINT

Nobody is born racist. Why do you think some people might grow up to have racist views?

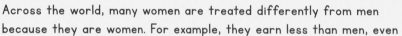

GENDER MATTERS

Did you know that for many people, their gender affects their power?

Across the world, many women are treated differently from men because they are women. For example, they earn less than men, even when they do the same job. Why does this happen? Part of the problem is **stereotypes**. A stereotype is the idea that someone should behave a certain way because they belong to a particular social group.

One stereotype is that boys don't cry. This means that as they grow up, boys are made to feel that they can't show their emotions. Another example of stereotyping is: Boys are AGGRESSIVE, girls are GENTLE. Is any of this true? Think about your friends and family.

I am a boy, so I can't cry.

I am a girl, so I can cry.

THINKING POINT

Look at the list of stereotypes below. Which ones do you recognize?

Can you think of any more?

- Girls like pink
- Girls like playing with dolls
- Women are better at cooking
- Nurses are women

- Boys like football
- Boys like playing with toy cars
- Men are better at math
- Mechanics are men

We are human beings and we get upset by stereotypes.

WHERE DID THESE STEREOTYPES COME FROM?

Long ago, life was much harder than it is today and physical strength was essential for survival. This meant that men often took more active roles, such as hunting or going to war, and this led to the belief that men were stronger than women in many ways. It meant that men rose to the top of governments, managed companies, and acted as heads of the family—in fact, they held all the power.

Today, things have changed for many people, but there are still millions of women and girls across the globe who don't have the same rights as men and boys and this limits their power to make choices. Some women can't choose who they want to marry and some girls aren't allowed to go to school.

THE GIRL WHO STOOD UP FOR HER EDUCATION

"One child, one teacher, one book, one pen can change the world."

Some people, such as **Malala Yousafzai**, challenge stereotypes. Malala was born in Pakistan in 1997 and went to school with other girls. However, when a group called the Taliban took over the area she lived in, girls were forbidden to go to school. When Malala spoke up against this, she was sought out and shot by the Taliban—but she survived. The attack didn't stop her from speaking out. Today, she campaigns to help girls all over the world become educated so that they are treated as equals to boys. This means they can learn and study and have a better chance to get the jobs they want when they are older.

RAINBOW RIGHTS

The people that you **love** should not affect the way that you are treated.

People can love each other in many ways. Romantic relationships can be between a woman and a man. Or, two people of the same gender—a woman and a woman, or a man and a man—can love each other.

A relationship between a woman and a man is known as **heterosexual**. A relationship between two people of the same gender is known as **homosexual**. A woman who is attracted to another woman is **lesbian**. A man who is attracted to another man is **gay**. Some people are attracted to both men and women—this is known as **bisexuality**.

Negative feelings toward gay people, such as hatred, fear, or prejudice, are known as homophobia. This can include the views that heterosexual relationships are "better" than homosexual ones, or that gay people are "unnatural" or not normal.

In many countries, gay people are not allowed to get married or have children, and are discriminated against at work and in society. In some countries, being homosexual is illegal, and gay people can be attacked violently or killed simply because of who they love.

LGBTQ RIGHTS

The **LGBTQ** movement fights for the rights of gay people and other people who don't fit into traditional gender roles. This includes people who feel they are a different gender to the one they were born in. Through activism and education, the movement aims to change people's attitudes and gain equal rights for everyone, everywhere. Its symbol is the rainbow flag.

THE NATIONAL HERO WHO WAS PUNISHED FOR BEING GAY

Born in 1912, the brilliant English mathematician Alan Turing is famous for breaking a secret code used by the Germans in World War II, and for his work on artificial intelligence (the intelligence shown by machines). In 1952, Turing was arrested and found guilty of the crime of being homosexual, which was against the law in Britain at the time. Because of this, his career was ruined, and he was no longer allowed to work for the government. Two years later, he killed himself. In 2013, nearly 60 years after his death, following a campaign by tens of thousands of people, Turing received a pardon from Queen Elizabeth II for his conviction.

THINKING POINT

Many fairytales feature a princess and a prince, who fall in love and live happily ever after. These stories are almost always about heterosexual love. But in real life, fairytale endings can happen between people of the same gender, too. Imagine if Snow White and Cinderella fell in love, for example. Do you think that would be a magical ending?

DIFFERENT BODIES

Disabled people are disabled by **the world around them** and not by their bodies.

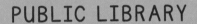

Some people have difficulties doing certain things, such as seeing, hearing, walking, speaking, or learning. This is called a disability.

What makes a person "disabled"? One way of thinking says disabled people are disabled not by their bodies, but by the world around them—for example by people's negative attitudes, or by places or activities that aren't accessible to everyone. This idea is called the Social Model of Disability.

Here are some examples of ways society can "disable" people who have problems doing certain things:

- **Movies or plays** shown without subtitles or a sign language interpreter can't be enjoyed by deaf people.

- **Buildings** without ramps or bathrooms for disabled people can't be used by wheelchair users.

- **Negative attitudes** that focus on what disabled people can't do make it harder for disabled people to work, live by themselves, or do certain things.

PUBLIC LIBRARY

The Social Model of Disability says that it is up to society to make changes, so that disabled people have the same power as able-bodied people to do the things they want to do. Being disabled doesn't mean you can't achieve amazing things.

THE MAN WHO EXPLORED THE UNIVERSE

> "However difficult life may seem, there is always something you can do and succeed at."

The British physicist **Stephen Hawking** is remembered as one of the most important scientists of the last century. He changed the way we understand how the universe works, and wrote several books that sold millions of copies worldwide and opened up science to everyone. Professor Hawking could not speak or move and had to be helped to do pretty much everything, but his disability did not hold him back. He used technology to write his books, become a media star, and add to the scientific knowledge of humanity. Using a wheelchair and technology enabled him to live his life as he wished, including getting married, having children, and enjoying a successful career. Just because he did things differently, it didn't make them any less amazing.

If you are disabled, never forget **there isn't anything you can't do**. You might do it differently—for example, Stephen Hawking wrote his books using technology that let him use eye movement to write rather than tapping keys on a keyboard—but you can still do it. Disabled people have trekked to the South Pole, sold millions of records, become professional dancers, surfers, and baseball players, won gold medals competing in sports, climbed Mount Everest, and even become President of the US.

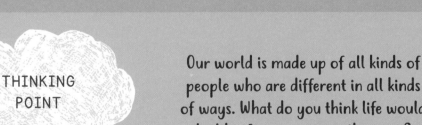

THINKING POINT

Our world is made up of all kinds of people who are different in all kinds of ways. What do you think life would be like if everyone was the same?

THE POWER OF MONEY

Having money gives you power,
but **money isn't everything.**

Around the world, people's opportunities to have a full and happy life are not equal. Some people have the power to affect the lives of millions. Other people don't even have control over their own lives.

This difference in power is partly due to money. Around 10 percent of the world's population live on less than $2 per day for their food, clothing, and housing. At the other end of the scale, the richest one percent of the world's population have half of all the money in the world.

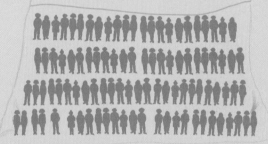

1% of the population have half the world's money.

99% of the population have the other half.

If a child is born in a **rich country**, he or she will go to school to get a good education, so that when they are older they can get a job and gain more skills. They will have clean water to drink, and when they are sick, they can quickly be taken to a doctor or to the hospital. A child born in a very **poor country** might not grow up with any of these advantages. Which child do you think will have more opportunities and power to make things happen in their life?

Even in rich countries, there are differences between the wealth that people have, and this can affect people's opportunities. Somebody who is rich has more choice about where they want to live and which school their children go to, for example.

SOLD

£

How do people become wealthy? Sometimes people inherit money from their parents, and sometimes they earn it themselves. Some of the richest people in the world started out with nothing, but had a good business idea and were determined and hard-working enough to make it succeed.

THE BILLIONAIRE WHO GIVES HIS MONEY AWAY

"The general idea of the rich helping the poor, I think, is important."

One of the world's richest people, the entrepreneur **Bill Gates**, is worth almost 100 billion (that's one thousand million) US dollars. Gates made his fortune himself. When he was 20, he and his schoolfriend, Paul Allen, founded Microsoft, which grew to become the biggest software company in the world. Gates has used some of his enormous wealth and power to try to change the world for the better. He and his wife set up the Bill & Melinda Gates Foundation, which has donated billions of dollars to charity. One of its main aims is to reduce extreme poverty and make the world a fairer place.

There are different ways you can be powerful. Having money gives you more opportunities, and often more power as a result, but it isn't everything. Even if you are very rich, people can still look down on you. And even if you have very little money, you might still have the power to influence the people around you by making them like or respect you, by being polite, funny, charming, kind, or helpful.

"The ultimate source of happiness is not money and power, but warm-heartedness."
The Dalai Lama

Do you agree?

THINKING POINT

45

INVISIBLE POWER

Do you ever stop to think about the
unwritten rules
that we all follow?

Some power is obvious, like the power of a person or an organization—your parents or your school, for example, or the police. But other power is invisible. We don't even realize it is there, but it still affects the way we all behave.

An example of this is something called "**social norms.**" These are basically unwritten rules about how to behave. Manners, such as saying please and thank you, are social norms. So is wearing the right clothes for a certain situation—for example, you wouldn't turn up at school wearing a swimsuit! If a person breaks the accepted rules of social norms, they might be looked down on or avoided, so we normally follow the rules because we all want to fit in.

Social norms are useful because they make people behave, but they can also discriminate against anyone who is seen as "abnormal." For example, think about the social norm in most Western countries that only girls wear skirts. Some boys may want to wear skirts too, but in many places they would be teased for this. In other cultures, however, it is the social norm that boys can wear skirts. In Scotland, for example, boys sometimes wear kilts, and in Bali in Indonesia, both boys and girls can wear a kamben, a skirt-like piece of fabric wrapped around the waist.

THINKING
POINT

What other social norms can you think of? Do you think they are good, or bad?

Social norms can be different in different cultures, and they can sometimes lead to discrimination against large groups of people. In some cultures, for example, the social norm is that girls are not as important as boys, so girls stay at home and look after the children or do housework while boys go to school, and grow up to hold positions of authority. A society where men, rather than women, hold the power is called a **patriarchy**.

Social norms are very powerful. They are invisible, so we tend not to question them and we accept that this is just the way things are. But, social norms can change. Things that were once seen as "abnormal," such as women being able to vote, for example, have become normal around the world.

THE SOCIETY WHERE WOMEN ARE IN CHARGE

A **matriarchy** is a society where women hold the power, rather than men. Most people agree that there are no real matriarchies in the world. However, there are some societies where the women have a lot of power. The Mosuo people, in China, are one example. Here, the women are head of the household and tell everyone what to do. They own the land and houses, and manage all of the money. Children are brought up by their mother—the father lives in a separate house.

"I am strong. I am kind.
I am unique. I believe in me."

YOUR POWER

So far in this book, we've looked at different types of power, how it can be used well, and how it can be used badly.

We've shared the stories of some inspiring and thought-provoking people who used, claimed, or challenged power.

We've explored how power affects us all in tiny and huge ways.

Now, in this chapter,
it's all about YOU!

WHAT'S YOUR POWER STYLE?

We all have power, but the way that we use that power varies.
This partly depends on personality, so try this quiz to
find out your power style!

START HERE!

Do you like to be the team leader?

YES →

Do you get along well with most people?

NO ↓

YES ↓

Do you get annoyed if you don't get your own way?

YES →

Do you like to make plans, or do you prefer to go along with what other people want to do?

NO ↓

GO ALONG WITH OTHERS

Do you feel confident when you have to stand up and talk in front of the rest of your class?

YES →

NO →

NO

YES

Do you prefer listening to talking?

Has anyone ever said you are a bit scary?

YES

NO

NO

YES

Are you good at organizing things, and making things happen?

NO

MAKE PLANS

Do people ever copy what you do, or what you wear?

YES

NO

NO

Are you sometimes teased for being a bit different, or not really cool?

YES

You are a BIG BOSS!

Your power style is very direct. You like to be in charge, and you are very good at getting other people organized. If things aren't going your way, you might sometimes get angry or shout at people. Remember, it's OK to be direct, and it's great that you get things done, but make sure you use your power kindly.

You are an INFLUENCER!

Like celebrities, you have power because people want to be like you. You are popular and cool, and even though you don't boss people around, they like to please you. But with great power comes great responsibility: make sure to be kind, because you are a role model who influences other people's behavior.

You are THE CHILLED ONE!

You are very easygoing, and are more likely to go along with what someone else wants to do than try and exert power over them. But this can be powerful in itself. The ancient Chinese philosopher Confucius said, "The green reed which bends in the wind is stronger than the mighty oak which breaks in a storm." If people can't upset you easily, that makes you strong. Just make sure you don't become a pushover.

EMPOWER YOURSELF

Learn how to **super-charge** your power!

As a child, you might feel that you don't have much power in your life. Parents tell you what to do at home, and teachers tell you what to do at school. But there are lots of ways you can boost your power.

One of the most important ways you can empower yourself is to have **self-esteem**. This means believing in yourself, being confident about your ideas and actions, and thinking good thoughts about yourself.

This can sometimes be a tricky thing to do. Try to think about occasions when you have done well, rather than times you have failed. Remember that your opinions matter just as much as anybody else's, and try not to care too much about what other people might think of you. Most importantly, be yourself!

BOOST YOUR SELF-ESTEEM, RIGHT NOW!

Write down three things you do well. This could be anything, from math or drawing, to running or singing, making people laugh, doing jigsaws, working hard, or being kind to your friends. We all have lots of different talents, and reminding ourselves what we are good at helps to raise our self-esteem.

MINDFULNESS MANTRA

A technique called **mindfulness** can also help us to have more positive thoughts about ourselves. Mindfulness just means giving our full attention to something. When we are being mindful, we notice how we are thinking and feeling and what is around us right now. Try starting every day with a Positive Thoughts Mantra. You could do this by yourself or with a parent. A mantra is just a word or words that are repeated. Sit somewhere quiet, and take a few deep breaths. Then say the following words to yourself, either out loud or silently in your head:

"I am strong. I am kind. I am unique. I believe in me."

Repeat this a few times, and make sure you really pay attention to the words as you say them. Think about how they make you feel. Does being positive about yourself make you feel powerful?

There are lots of ways you can try to make sure that the power around you is used fairly and kindly. At school, you can do your best to always act with kindness and respect toward others. Believe in yourself and feel confident to say what you think, but also listen to the ideas of others. If you see power being used unfairly, for example by bullies, stand up for the person being bullied or let a teacher know.

At home, you could suggest that everyone sits down together to decide on some family rules. Or you could organize a regular family meeting, where everyone gets the chance to talk about their ideas and feelings. You could even all take turns leading the meeting!

LEARN MORE, THINK MORE

Knowledge is power.

One way you can have more power in your life is to learn more and think more about the world around you. The more knowledge you have, the more power you have to make up your own mind about things—and maybe one day change them.

How much do you know about how the government works in your country, for example? Who is in power, and how does that power work? Who is in charge in your local neighborhood? The people in charge of your country make all sorts of decisions that affect YOU, from the subjects you are taught at school to what age you will be allowed to drive, vote, start working, and eventually retire. When you are reading or listening to the news, think about which issues are important to you. After all, you will be voting one day. You never know—you might even end up running the country!

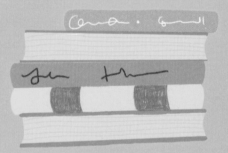

You can get knowledge from lots of different places. You can read books, go online, watch the news on TV, and talk to your family, friends, teachers, and other people. The more you can read and talk and listen and think, the better!

Who runs my country?

When can I vote?

HOW TO DEBATE

A **debate** is a discussion about a particular topic or issue. You might find that you don't always agree with other people's views about things, and that's fine. Here are some tips on how to argue your views without upsetting the other person.

- Back up your argument with lots of facts—the more you read and listen and learn, the more facts you will have, and the stronger your argument will be!

- Always stay polite and don't lose your temper.

- Listen to what the other person has to say. You never know, you might even end up changing your mind...

Reading and talking to people is important. But don't assume that everything you read or are told is right! Being able to **think for yourself** is an important skill. It's helpful to listen to different viewpoints from different people; then you can make up your own mind about what YOU think is right.

How can we look after the world?

When we learn more and think more about the world around us, we become more aware of things that may not be fair or right. We might notice that certain groups of people are being treated unfairly, for example, or we might question some of the social norms we take for granted. Thinking about the world around us is the first step to making it better.

Is everyone treated fairly?

SPREAD THE WORD

Use your power to
make change!

When you look at the world around you, there might be things that you don't think are right or fair. This could be something close to home, like your local library closing down, or it might be something that affects the whole planet, such as the destruction of the Amazon rain forest. What should you do? You could just accept the problem, or wait for someone in power to solve it. Or you could try to do something about it yourself.

An organized plan that tries to achieve a particular goal is called a **campaign**. How does a campaign work? It uses the power of a group, working together, to make change. Here is an example.

You have read about plastic waste and the harm it is doing to sea life. You decide to stop buying plastic water bottles.

Next, you spread the word. You persuade your friends and family to stop buying plastic bottles, too. At school, you tell your class about your campaign.

Everybody gets behind it and soon the whole school becomes a plastic-free zone. The media get involved and more and more people join the campaign. If enough people stop buying plastic bottles, harmful plastics might eventually be banned and replaced by new, safer material.

CAMPAIGN TOOLBOX!

There are lots of different tools you can
use in a campaign.

LETTERS Writing a letter can be a powerful way
to let people in charge know how you feel about an
issue. For example, you might be unhappy about the
way that many girls' toys are colored pink and boys'
toys are blue. If enough people write to the people
who make the toys, explaining why they think this is
wrong, the manufacturers might change
the way they do things.

THE MEDIA You can bring your campaign's
message to a larger number of people by
getting the local media involved. You could, for
example, invite a local newspaper to come and
talk to you about your campaign.

PETITIONS A petition is a request to somebody to
do something, which is signed by lots of people. For
example, you could organize a petition in your local
neighborhood to increase the number of recycling
bins on the streets. The more signatures you are
able to collect, the more power your petition will
have when you present it to your local council.

POSTERS AND LEAFLETS You can spread
the word about your campaign by putting
up posters and handing out leaflets. This
educates other people about the issue.
Keep your message simple: a picture can
be more powerful than lots of words.

BE INSPIRED!

No matter how old you are,

YOU

have the power to change the world.

You might think that because you're a child you don't have any power, and that you're too young to make a difference to the world. But that's not true.

We've already seen how the young activist Malala Yousafzai (see page 39) has campaigned for the rights of girls to have an education. At the age of 17, Malala became the youngest person in history to receive the Nobel Peace Prize—one of the world's most important awards. Here you can read about other young people around the world who have fought for something they believed in and made a difference.

Read their stories and be inspired. If they can do it, YOU can, too!

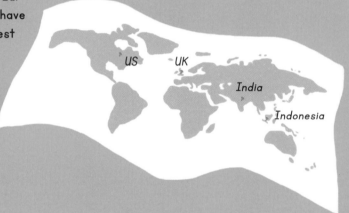

US   UK
India
Indonesia

Melati and **Isabel Wijsen** were just 10 and 12 when they started their campaign in 2013 to tackle plastic pollution on their home island of Bali, in Indonesia. Inspired by a lesson at school about activism, the sisters started a petition to ban plastic bags, and collected 100,000 signatures. Eventually, their campaigning work persuaded the governor of Bali to commit to making the island plastic free. Hundreds of stores in Bali have stopped using plastic bags, and tens of thousands of people have volunteered for beach clean-ups. The sisters' organization, Bye Bye Plastic Bags, has grown into an international youth movement with groups in 25 countries.

In 2015, 11-year-old American **Marley Dias** complained to her mother that most of the books she read were about white boys or dogs. She launched a campaign called #1000BlackGirlBooks, which aimed to collect and donate 1,000 books that had black girls as the main characters. She ended up with over 9,000 books, and her campaign brought attention to the issue of including different types of people in children's books.

Having suffered years of bullying at school, 15-year-old British schoolboy **Liam Hackett** set up a forum on the internet in 2006 where people could share their own experiences of bullying. He turned this into an actual website, Ditch the Label, the following year. After finishing college, Liam set up the Ditch the Label anti-bullying charity, which runs campaigns and offers online support. Today the charity works in the UK, US, and Mexico, and has helped hundreds of thousands of young people.

In Rajasthan, India, in 2013, 12-year-old **Payal Jangid** was chosen to lead her village's "children's parliament"—a group of children who meet to share ideas and suggest better ways of doing things. The village where she lived was very poor. Not all children went to school and some girls were forced to get married while they were still young. Payal fought to improve children's rights in her community. Working with others, she organized talks and rallies, and even went from door to door persuading parents to send their children to school. Her work helped to change attitudes in her village and improve the lives of children.

GLOSSARY

A **abolitionist** A person who works to end slavery.

activism Actions, such as demonstrations or petitions, which aim to bring about changes in society.

activist Someone who deliberately acts to bring about change.

B **ballot paper** A piece of paper used for voting. The voter chooses who they want to win from a list of names.

C **campaign** A series of organized actions that aims to bring about a particular result.

censorship The banning of certain information by a government or group, for example stopping certain books or newspapers from being published, or preventing people from speaking.

citizen A person who lives in a country or state and legally belongs to it.

civil rights The right for every person to be treated equally and fairly.

D **demonstration** A meeting of a group of people, such as a march, to protest against something or show their support of something.

discrimination The unfair treatment of a person or group of people, for example because of their race, sex, disability, or religion.

E **election** A process where people vote to choose a person for an official (often political) position.

empowerment The aim to improve a person's life by giving them the knowledge, confidence, and strength to make a positive change.

equality A state where everyone is equal, and has the same rights and opportunities.

exploitation Treating or using a person unfairly, in order to gain from their work.

G **gender** The characteristics that are related to being male or female. Gender isn't always about a person's physical body, but can be about how they feel inside. For some people, their body doesn't match with the gender that they feel. This is called being transgender. Some people feel that they aren't a single gender. This is called being non-binary.

government The people who govern, or control, a country or state.

H **hierarchy** The way things or people are organized into levels, depending on how important they are, with the most important at the top.

L **LGBTQ** These initials stand for lesbian, gay, bisexual, transgender, and queer or questioning (for people who are unsure of their gender or sexuality).

M **modern slavery** The many forms of slavery that still exist in the world today, such as when people are forced to work against their will.

N **nation** A group of people living in a particular place, who share the same history, language, or culture.

P **petition** A request from a group of people to a government or organization, asking them to do something. It is often signed by lots of people.

prejudice An unfair opinion about something or someone that is decided in advance and isn't based on fact.

privilege Special rights that only a particular person or group has.

propaganda The spreading of one-sided information that is intended to persuade people to think or feel a particular way.

protest An action to express an objection to something.

R **rallies** Large gatherings in a public place where people join together to support something they all believe in.

rebellion The rising up against a government or ruler.

resources Materials or wealth that can be used by people. A country's natural resources include precious minerals, forests, oil, and gas.

revolution The successful overthrow of a government or monarch, often by force.

rights The freedom to do certain things, such as vote, go to school or live in safety.

S **sabotage** The act of deliberately destroying property or equipment, for example as a protest or in a war.

segregation The deliberate act of keeping apart different groups of people, for example because of their race.

social media Websites and apps that allow people to communicate with each other and share information.

society A large community of people living in a particular place, such as a country, who share laws, traditions, and organizations.

T **tyrant** A ruler who has complete power and often uses it in a cruel way.

TAKING IT FURTHER

- *Culture and Diversity (I'm a Global Citizen series)*
  By Georgia Amson-Bradshaw
  Franklin Watts, 2019

- *Dream Big! Heroes Who Dared to be Bold*
  By Sally Morgan
  Scholastic, 2019

- *Feminism is...*
  By various authors
  DK, 2019

- *How Money Works: The Facts Visually Explained*
  By various authors
  DK, 2017

- *Little Leaders: Bold Women in Black History*
  By Vashti Harrison
  Little Brown Young Readers, 2017

- *Little Leaders: Visionary Women Around the World*
  By Vashti Harrison
  Little Brown Young Readers, 2018

- *Mindful Me: Mindfulness and Meditation for Kids*
  By Whitney Stewart
  Albert Whitman & Company, 2018

- *Politics for Beginners*
  By various authors
  Usborne, 2018

- *Queer Heroes*
  By Arabelle Sicardi
  Wide Eyed Editions, 2019

- *Rebel Voices: The Rise of Votes for Women*
  By Louise Kay Stewart
  Hachette Children's Group, 2018

- *Speak Up!*
  By Laura Coryton
  Red Shed, 2019

- *Step Into Your Power*
  by Jamia Wilson
  Wide Eyed Editions, 2019

- *You Are Awesome: Find Your Confidence
  and Dare to be Brilliant at (Almost) Anything*
  By Matthew Syed
  Wren & Rook, 2018

- *Young, Gifted and Black*
  By Jamia Wilson
  Wide Eyed Editions, 2018

 IF YOU FEEL UNSAFE AT HOME
OR AT SCHOOL, CONTACT
WWW.CHILDHELP.ORG

ABOUT THE CONTRIBUTORS

Claire Saunders lives in Lewes, UK, where she works as a writer and editor. She has two children, Tom and Mia, whom she hopes will grow up believing in themselves and their power to change the world.

Hazel Songhurst writes and edits nonfiction on a wide range of topics for children of all ages. She believes in the power of books to inform and inspire the grownups of the future.

Georgia Amson-Bradshaw is a children's writer and editor from Brighton, UK. She has been trying to use her power to change the world since she was six years old, when she started the Children's Earth Saver's Club. As a grownup, she studied how media can impact social change, and now makes books that aim to make the world a better, fairer place.

Minna Salami is a writer and lecturer, and the founder of the award-winning blog, *MsAfropolitan*, which connects feminism with critical reflections on contemporary culture from an Africa-centred perspective. She is a contributor to *The Guardian*, CNN, and the BBC, as well as a speaker for the EU and the UN.

Mik Scarlet is a writer and broadcaster based in London, UK. He is an expert in the field of access and inclusion for disabled people.

Joelle Avelino is a Congolese and Angolan illustrator, based in London, UK. She believes that every child should be able to see themselves in the books that they read. Joelle's biggest inspiration is her daughter, Zaina-Marie.

David Broadbent lives in Brighton, UK, and has been an illustrator for nearly 20 years. He has worked on many books that encourage young people to be the change that they want to see in the world.